Qu
Tea
m
simple
FOR MEN

Edited by
Saniyasnain Khan

Goodword

The text in this book is gleaned from
*The Quran: English Translation, Commentary and Parallel Arabic
Text* by Maulana Wahiduddin Khan
Edited by Farida Khanam, Goodword Books, 2011.

Art Editor: Mohd. Noman Khan
Project Editor: Maria Khan
Research: Mohd. Harun Rashid
Design: K.K. Sahadevan

First published 2011
Reprinted 2013
© Goodword Books 2013

Goodword Books
1, Nizamuddin West Market, New Delhi-110 013
Mob. +91-8588822672
Tel. +9111-4182-7083, 4652-1511
email: info@goodwordbooks.com
www.goodwordbooks.com

Islamic Vision Ltd.
434 Coventry Road, Small Heath
Birmingham B10 0UG, U.K.
Tel. 121-773-0137
e-mail: info@ipci-iv.co.uk, www.islamicvision.co.uk

IB Publisher Inc.
81 Bloomingdale Rd, Hicksville, NY 11801, USA
Tel. 516-933-1000, Toll Free: 1-888-560-3222
email: info@ibpublisher.com, www.ibpublisher.com

Picture credits:
Mehmet Akif Guler: 64,
Goodword Books: 28, 29, 46, 47,
Rest of the images used
under license from 123rf.com

Printed in India

Contents

•••

This Quran guides to the best path, and brings good news to the believers who lead a righteous life, that they have deserved a great recompense. (*Al-Isra'* 17:9)

The Characteristics of a Believer

"True believers are those whose hearts tremble with awe at the mention of God, and whose faith grows stronger as they listen to His revelations. They are those who put their trust in their Lord, who pray regularly and give in alms out of what We have provided for them. Such are the true believers. They have a high standing with their Lord, His forgiveness and an honourable provision made for them." (*Al-Anfal* 8:2-4)

Faith is the discovery of the greatest reality. When this reality enters into any one's heart, it shakes one's whole personality. The state of one so affected is that when he is reminded of a truth, he immediately accepts it. Discovering God as Omnipotent naturally engenders within him the quality of trust.

Higher qualities of every kind naturally come into existence in such a person. He becomes, on the one hand, a true devotee of God and, on the other hand a true friend and well-wisher of other human beings.

Discovering God along with His greatness and glory is not a simple matter. This is a discovery such as effaces all feelings of superiority and arrogance from a man. It makes him a believer in the true sense of the word. And the other name of a true believer is a true human being.

Dawah Work

"O Prophet, We have sent forth you as a witness, as a bearer of good news and a warner. As one who calls people to God by His leave, and guides them like a shining light. Convey to the believers the good news that God has bounteous blessings in store for them."
(*Al-Ahzab* 33:45-47)

The witness (*shahid*), the bearer of good news (*mubashshir*), the warner, (*nadhir*) and the giver of the call for the Truth (*da'i*) all represent different aspects of the same reality. It is the Prophet's mission to make people aware of the realities of life and inform them about heaven and hell. This is an action related to the call of the Prophet and on this basis only, will the Prophet give evidence in the Court of the Hereafter as to which of his addressees accepted the message of Truth, and which did not.

The Prophet's mission is also the mission of the followers of Islam. While treading this path, one has to face trouble from the people in getting support; while some give timely support, they later desert, uttering falsehoods. Under these circumstances, it was Trust in God alone which kept the Prophet (or his follower-missionaries) firmly on the true path of their missionary work. To be tolerant of whatever is negative in the people, to ignore it and under all circumstances to keep one's eyes fixed on God: these are the real assets of one who performs work.

The Inevitability of the Hereafter

O believers! Do not let your wealth or your children distract you from remembrance of God. Those who do so will be the losers. And spend out of what We have provided you with before death comes to one of you and he says, 'My Lord! If only You would grant me respite for a little while, then I would give alms and be among the righteous.' But God will not grant a reprieve to a soul when its appointed time has come; God is well-aware of what you do. (*Al-Munafiqun* 63:9-11)

The biggest problem for a man is the inevitability of the Hereafter. But the consideration of riches and children make a man unmindful of it. Man should know that riches and children are not the final goal but the blessings which are given to him so that he may utilise them for God's work. He should therefore use them to improve his life in the Hereafter. But man, in his stupidity, takes them to be his goal. When such people come face to face with their eventual final fate, they will experience only frustration and regret.

Comfort for the Heart

> "Those who believe and whose hearts find comfort in the remembrance of God – surely in the remembrance of God hearts can find comfort."
> (*Al-Ra'd* 13:28).

What is comfort of the heart? It is the solace a man feels when he achieves what he wanted to achieve. On the contrary, discomfort of the heart is felt when a man is deprived of whatever he had a desire in his heart to achieve.

The things of this world in which a man seeks comfort besides that which God can give him, are all limited and imperfect. They do not measure up to actual human cravings. That is why the achieving of worldly or material things cannot satisfy a man. Before achieving these things the individual is very hopeful about them. But, after achieving them, his hopes come to naught. He enters a state in which the achievement or non-achievement of these things make no difference to him.

But the case of seeking and finding God is totally different from that. When a man discovers God, he feels that he has been given a complete response to his supplication. When a man remembers God and his relations with Him are established on a spiritual level, this amounts to complete fulfillment for his entire personality. When he ponders over the signs of the universe, he finds a response to his intellectual needs. This is that supreme experience, which is expressed in this verse as 'comfort of the heart.'

Usefulness

He sends down water from the sky that fills riverbeds to overflowing, each according to its measure. The torrent carries along swelling form, akin to what rises from smelted ore from which man makes ornaments and tools. God thus depicts truth and falsehood. The scum is cast away, but whatever is of use to man remains behind. God thus speaks in parable (*Al-Ra'd* 13:17).

In this verse, a law of nature has been explained in the form of a parable. This law says that only those can achieve stability and permanency who prove their usefulness. Those who cannot do so will find no place in this world of God.

An individual has to be useful to his family. Similarly, he has to be useful to his society. Without benefiting others, he will find a place of respect neither in the family nor in society. This is also true of national and international life. Here too, only those will be accorded respect who can prove their utility.

There are two types of usefulness– one in the material sense and the other in the moral sense. But the greatest benefit that a group or an individual can offer others is to present them with the gift of truth.

The World is not the Real Aim

— •••

> We give whatever We will to whoever
> desires immediate gains; but then We
> have prepared Hell for him which
> he will enter, disgraced and rejected.
> Anyone who desires the Hereafter and
> makes a proper effort to achieve it,
> being a true believer, shall find favour
> with God for his endeavours.
>
> Upon all, both these [who desire
> the world] and those [who desire the
> Hereafter] We bestow the bounty of
> your Lord: none shall be denied the
> bounty of your Lord. (*Al-Isra'* 17:18-20)

One can live his life in two ways: one of them is achieving
the world by worldly means, and the other is achieving the
Hereafter while in this world. Both these opportunities are
equally open to all people. It is man's duty to make a choice.
Man has been endowed with excellent physical and intellectual
capabilities. Moreover, in the outer world, all types of resources
are available in abundance. One who makes either of the above
two objectives his target, is instantly supported by all kinds of
resources.

This situation often creates misunderstanding in the mind
of an individual. Seeing the situation in his favour, he comes
to the conclusion that what he is doing is right. But this is
where a man is tested. He should not think himself to be right
only because he is seemingly advancing towards success and
progress. Every individual should make the truth his standard
and in its light decide whether he is on the right or wrong path.

Patience and Trust

> "We shall lodge forever those who believe and do good works in the mansions of Paradise beside which rivers flow. How excellent is the reward of those who labour, and who are steadfast and put their trust in their Lord."
> (*Al-'Ankabut* 29:58-59)

According to these verses, Paradise is for those individuals who have two types of moral qualities – patience and trust: these two qualities are the price of Paradise. Without these two qualities no one will be allowed to enter Paradise. The fact is that Paradise has always been for that sublime person who can provide proof in this world that he is possessed of a positive, divine personality.

The present world is designed in such a way that here the individual has to bear with unpleasant experiences. These bitter experiences repeatedly disturb a man's inner spiritual peace, making him repeatedly fall a prey to negative feelings. In such a situation, only those individuals can maintain their inner spirituality who have the extraordinary quality of patience; who are not affected by negative situations; who can provide the proof of living their lives on the principle of unilateral ethics. Such people are called patient.

The quality of trust protects a man from being shaken. It gives him a confident, trustful life. In this present world a man repeatedly faces such discouraging experiences as shake his inner personality. Sometimes he feels that others have more than he has. At other times he thinks that the resources he has are very inferior in relation to his ambitions. Sometimes it seems to him that certain situations are leading him to discouragement. This being so, only trust in God can support him. He can make progress in such unfavourable situations only by putting his trust on God. This trust is a unique, divine quality. That is why trust in God makes a man entitled to Paradise.

The Basis of Truth

"And still those who are unjust follow their own desires without having any knowledge. Then who can guide those whom God has let go astray? There shall be none to help them." (*Al-Rum* 30:29)

This verse tells us that the basis of truth is knowledge and the basis of falsehood is desire. In the present world the sources of guidance are so many that a man who is sincere and a true seeker of truth cannot fail to discover the truth. His own nature, his God-given reason, the signs spread all over the universe and God's Book are sufficient for the right guidance of a man.

Only that man will fail to discover the truth who, by ignoring the facts, comes to follow his own whims and desires. He comes to prefer the present world to the next world. He comes to attach more importance to his own interests than to principle. He comes to give preference to his interests over the truth. It is such people who will be deprived of the discovery of the truth.

The Religion of Nature

• • •

"Devote yourself single mindedly to the Religion. And follow the nature as made by God, that nature is which He has created mankind. There is no altering the creation of God. That is the right religion. But most people do not realize it turn to him and fear Him, and be steadfast in prayer, and do not be one of those who associate partners with God, those who split up their religion and became divided into sects; each one exulting in what they have."
(*Al-Rum* 30:32)

God's religion is innate in man's nature. And the nature of man is synonymous with God's religion. Hence, neither is the recognition of God's religion difficult for man nor is his living his life according to it. Despite all this, a man may stray, but then he himself is responsible for it.

The fact is that the true religion is one. And it was sent to each prophet in its complete form. That is: turning to one God, fear of one God, worship of one God and being devoted to one God. This is the religion of nature. This religion is eternally embedded in human psychology. All the prophets have taught this religion. But the later generations of their followers divided this religion into many religions.

The God-oriented Life

"He who submits himself completely to God, and is a doer of good, has surely grasped a strong handle, for the final outcome of all events rests with God. But if any reject the faith, let not his rejection grieve you: for to Us they shall return, and We shall tell them the truth about their deeds; for God knows well all that is in the human hearts – We shall let them enjoy themselves for a little while, but then We shall drive them to a harsh punishment." (*Luqman* 31:24)

Every man has a direction to which he always remains attentive with his entire intellectual and material existence. The believer is the one whose direction has turned totally towards God. The life of faith is the God-oriented life and the life without faith is the non-God-oriented life.

One who has directed himself towards God has actually set his foot on the right path. He will surely come to a good end. On the contrary, one who has become oblivious of God and directed himself towards someone or something else has lost his orientation as well as failing to reach his destination. He can receive some benefits in this present world but, in the eternal life of the hereafter, nothing but torment will await him.

The Lesson of the Universe

●●●

> "We did not create heaven and earth and all that is between them in vain. That is the opinion of those who deny the truth. Woe betide those who deny the truth, when they are cast into the Fire— shall We treat those who believe and do good works the same as those who spread corruption in the land; shall We treat the pious the same as the wicked?"
> (*Sad* 38:27-28)

After deep reflection on the mechanism of the world, we come to know that its whole system stands on very wise bases, although it was also possible that it was a random system in which nothing had any certainty. The existence of the more fitting of the two possibilities indicates that its Creator erected this world a result of purposeful planning. And how can that world be purposeless in its final stage which is so purposeful in its initial stage?

Every man in this world is free and independent. Observation shows that there are always some of the people who acknowledge the truth of their own free will and make themselves subservient to that truth. On the other hand, there are some who do not acknowledge the truth. They say whatever they want and act however they like without any restriction. Human reason does not accept that both types of people will meet the same end.

On taking an overview of the world's situation it is evident that, the statements of the Quran about human life come closer to reality than the statements of those who try to interpret life in a way just the opposite of that. The Quran is a divine annunciation of the truths of the universe and its being in conformity with reality is substantial evidence of its being true.

Worship of God

"God is the Creator of all things, He has charge of everything; the keys of the heavens and the earth belong to Him. Those who deny God's revelations will surely be the losers. Say, 'Ignorant men! Would you bid me worship someone other than God?' It has already been revealed to you and to those who have gone before you that if you ascribe any partner to God, all your works will come to nothing, and you will surely be among the losers. Therefore, you should worship God alone and be among the thankful."
(*Al-Zumar* 39:62-66)

The existence of the universe is in itself evidence of the existence of its Creator. Similarly, its functioning in a very meaningful and systematic way is evidence of the fact that a Watcher is constantly watching it. If a man gives this deep thought, he will find the Creator's design immanent in this universe.

In this situation, those who worship other gods other than the one God are doing something which has no value in this present universe. Since the Creator and Nourisher is one, worshipping Him alone can benefit a man. Worshipping someone or something else is like calling upon a deity who has no existence at all.

The World and the Hereafter

"God is most Gracious to His creatures: He provides sustenance for whoever He wills—for He alone is the Powerful One, the Almighty. To him who desires a harvest in the life to come, We shall grant an increase in his harvest; whereas to him who desires [but] a harvest in this world, We [may] give something thereof—but he will have no share in [the blessings of] the life to come."
(*Al-Shura* 42:19-20)

The life of this world is a test. Here, everyone is provided with the resources necessary for the test. Now, one who is Hereafter-loving will use the resources of this world in building the Hereafter. As a result, he will get his reward in the Hereafter.

On the contrary, one who is world-loving will act to derive advantage from the present world. Such a man can receive the fruits of his labour in the present world but, in the life of the hereafter, he will be a totally deprived person.

Meaningfulness of the Universe

"We did not idly create the heavens and the earth and all that lies between them; We did not create them save with a purpose, yet most people have no knowledge of this. Truly, the Day of Decision is the appointed time for all of them, the Day when no friend shall be of the least avail to another, nor shall any be helped, save those to whom God shows mercy. Surely, He is the Mighty, the Merciful One." (*Al-Dhukan* 44:38-42)

If we ponder upon the system of earth and sky, we will come to know that its creation has been done in a very meaningful way. The whole universe functions for a purpose. If the system of this universe did not have this meaningfulness, the development of any great civilization in this world would become impossible for human beings.

The Faith in the hereafter is an extension of the meaningfulness of the universe. It is impossible for this universe, which has been created in so meaningful way, to end in a total meaningless way. The present meaningfulness of the universe is indicative of the fact that its end will be meaningful and purposeful. The hereafter is the other name of this meaningful and purposeful end. The present stage of the world is one of trial. So, today every man is receiving his share of the meaningfulness of the universe. But when Doomsday comes, only those will have their share in this meaningfulness who are declared by God to be entitled to it.

A Meaningful End

"Do those who commit evil deeds imagine that We shall deal with them in the same way as We deal with those who have attained to faith and do righteous deeds, that they will be alike in their living and their dying? How badly they judge! God has created the heavens and the earth for a true purpose, so that every soul may be rewarded for whatever it has earned, and no one will be wronged." (*Al-Jathiyah* 45:21-22)

One who thinks that doing good and bad is equal, just as one day is like another and that both the one who does good as well as the one who does evil will have to die and be obliterated is senseless in his thinking. Such thinking is against that just consciousness which existed in human nature since birth. Such thinking, moreover, denies that meaningfulness of the universe which exists in its system in perfect form. The fact is that the inner nature of man and the vast eternal universe both prove it to be totally wrong that life could have been conceived as a purposeless thing with no meaningful end.

Great Success

"We have given you abundance. Pray to your Lord and sacrifice to Him alone. It is the one who hates you who has been cut off." (*Al-Kawthar* 108:1-3)

The Prophet brought the message of unadulterated truth. This is the most difficult task of the present world. The Prophet had to lose his all in order to preach this message. He was alienated from his community and his livelihood was destroyed. The future of his children became dark. Except for only a few, no one supported him. But in these discouraging situations, a revelation came down from God: We have given you abundance (*kauthar*), i.e. every type of supreme success. In the later years, this entire prediction of the Quran came true.

The same promise holds for the followers of the Prophet stage by stage. They can also achieve 'abundant goodness' but the condition is that they should propagate the same unadulterated religion which was brought to them by the Prophet and his companions. This abundant goodness carries on from this world to the next. It will never come to an end. If a right mission is faltering in its initial stages, it should not be imagined that it will always remain in this same condition. A right mission is always backed by God and, finally, it will achieve success.

Greed for More and More

...

"Greed for more and more distracted you [from God] till you reached the grave. But you will soon come to know. But you will soon come to know. Indeed, were you to know the truth with certainty, you would see the fire of Hell. You would see it with the eye of certainty. Then on that Day you shall be questioned about your worldly favours." (*Al-Takathur* 102:1-8)

Man desires to earn more and more wealth; to accumulate more and more comforts and luxuries of the world. He remains obsessed with this same craze until death draws near, then at that time he comes to know that what had to be accumulated was something other that what he had remained busy in accumulating. Any increase in worldly things only increases man's responsibilities, while man thinks foolishly that he is increasing in his success. Undoubtedly, this is the greatest misconception on the part of man.

Comfort and Discomfort

● ● ●

"As for man, when his Lord tests him, through honour and blessings, he says, 'My Lord has honoured me,' but when He tests him by straitening his means of livelihood, he says, 'My Lord has disgraced me.' No indeed, but you show no kindness to the orphan, nor do you urge one another to feed the poor, and you greedily devour the inheritance of the weak, and you have a love of wealth which can never be satisfied."
(*Al-Fajr* 89:15-29)

In this world, man is faced with two types of situations – losing and gaining. Both these situations are meant as tests. They are meant to test how a man reacts in a particular situation. The man who, when blessed with something, becomes arrogant and, when deprived of some favour, falls a prey to negative feelings, has failed in the test.

Another type of man is the one who, when he has received a favour from God, thanks Him and when deprived of something, bows down to Him, accepting his powerlessness. It is the latter type of man who is called here *mutma'innah,* or soul at peace. The status of *nafs mutma'innah* is accorded to those who ponder over the signs of God in the universe; who can take lessons from the events of history; who provide proof of the fact that, when there is a clash between truth and his own self, he will ignore his own self and accept the truth; who once having accepted the truth, will never forsake it, even if as a result his life becomes desolate.

The Success of Humanity

"He who purifies himself, who remembers the name of his Lord and prays, shall indeed be successful. But you prefer the life of this world, although the Hereafter is better and more lasting. This indeed is what is taught in the former scriptures— the scriptures of Abraham and Moses."
(*Al-A'la* 87:14-19)

God's religion has always been the same. The religion God revealed in the Quran is also the religion of the earlier prophets. The difference between the last Prophet and earlier prophets with regard to *Minhaj* and *Shir'ah* is only relative and not real. This type of relative difference is found in different situations of one and the same prophet, for example, the difference in the ordinances governing prayer and fasting in the Makkan and Medinan periods of the Prophet.

The true religion of God was revealed to all the prophets. This being so, human success depends on the fact that a man, by purifying himself, makes himself God's desired servant. This is a task of self-building, and only those can be successful in this world who, avoiding the transitory interests of the present world, make the next world the objects of their preference.

The Future of Man

"Believers! Fear God, and let every soul look to what it lays up for the future. Fear God: God is aware of what you do. Do not be like those who forgot God, so that He caused them to forget their own souls [their own true interests]. It is they who are the rebellious ones. The people of the Fire and the people of Paradise are not equal. The people of Paradise are the victorious ones." (*Al-Hashr* 59:18-20)

Human life has been divided into 'today' and 'tomorrow'. The present world is man's today while the next world is man's tomorrow. What a man does in this present world will yield its result in the hereafter.

This is the truth, the other name for which is Islam. Man's success lies in his always keeping this fact in his mind. One who is oblivious of this fact will find his whole life ultimately destroyed.

In this regard, there is no difference between Muslims and non-Muslims. Muslims can profit from the above knowledge but only if they really follow it. If they are negligent, they will meet the same end as the Jews met due to their negligence in previous times.

In the hereafter a differentiation will be made between successful and unsuccessful people. The former group will enter paradise while the latter group will be thrown into the fire of Hell. This will not be done on a social or group basis. It will be done on the basis of fact. Everyone's future will be decided on his own merit rather than on the basis of any hypothesis.

Successful Business

• • •

"Believers! Shall I guide you to a profitable course that will save you from a painful punishment? You should believe in God and His Messenger, and strive for God's cause with your possessions and your lives. That will be better for you, if you only knew— and He will forgive you your sins and admit you into Gardens with rivers flowing under them. He will lodge you in fine dwellings in the Gardens of Eternity; that is indeed the supreme achievement. He will give you another blessing which you desire: help from God and imminent victory. Give good tidings [O Muhammad] to believers!"
(*Al-Saff* 61:10-13)

In a business a man first invests, then makes profits. In a religious struggle also a man has to expend his wealth and energy. This is, so to speak, a kind of business. However, one can reap the benefits of worldly business only in this world whereas one can have the benefits of the 'business' of religion in this world as well as in the hereafter.

A Goodly Loan

"Your Lord knows that you stand up praying for nearly two-thirds of the night, or one-half of it and sometimes one third of it, as do others among your followers. God determines the measure of night and day. He knows that you will not be able to do it, so He has turned to you in mercy. Recite, then, as much of the Quran as is easy for you. He knows that there will be some among you who may be sick and others who will be travelling throughout the land seeking God's bounty, and yet others who may be fighting for the cause of God. So, recite, then as much of it as you are able, and be constant in prayer, and spend in charity, and give to God a goodly loan. For whatever good deed you send on before you for your souls, you will find it with God. It will be improved and richly rewarded by Him. Seek God's forgiveness, He is most forgiving, most merciful."
(*Al-Muzzammil* 73:20)

The obligatory duties of the religion have been laid down, keeping in view the capacity of the common man. But these duties enumerate only the compulsory limitations. Beyond these compulsory limitations, there are other desired actions, which are supererogatory: for example, the *tahajjud* prayer, besides the daily five times obligatory prayers, spending one's wealth for a good cause besides compulsory charity, or *zakat*, *umrah* besides the compulsory hajj etc. The test of a man's courage is how many such actions he performs. This also determines how many rewards he becomes entitled to.

The phrase 'goodly loan' does not pertain only to worship but also to other religious duties. For example, in ethical matters, behaving with a man in a better way than he has behaved with others. Similarly, in *dawah* activities, spending one's time and energy without any expectation of any recompense etc. The true believer is the one whose actions – including those which are supererogatory – all deserve to be called a 'goodly loan'.

Conscience

"By the Day of Resurrection, and by the self-reproaching soul! Does man think that We cannot [resurrect him and] bring his bones together again? Indeed, We have the power to restore his very finger tips! Yet man wants to deny what is ahead of him: he asks, 'When is this Day of Resurrection to be?' But [on that Day], when mortal sight is confounded, and the moon is eclipsed, when the sun and the moon are brought together, on that Day man will ask, 'Where can I escape?' But there is nowhere to take refuge: on that Day, to your Lord alone is the recourse. On that Day, man will be told of all that he has sent before and what he has left behind. Indeed, man shall be a witness against himself, in spite of all the excuses he may offer." (*Al-Qiyamah* 75:1-15)

Man has been endowed from birth with the ability to distinguish between right and wrong. As a result, he understands that the wrong-doers must be punished and the righteous rewarded. It is this consciousness which is called *nafs lawwamah*, or conscience, in the Quran. This conscience is psychological evidence of the reality of the hereafter. In the light of this inner evidence, one who does not fulfil its requirements is as if denying his own nature. In this verse, what is meant by *nafs lawwamah* is that which is generally called conscience. This conscience has been gifted uniquely to human beings. Apparently, animals are also creatures like human beings but no animal has a quality like the conscience. The exceptional existence of a thing like the conscience in the human being proves that the case of human beings is entirely different from that of other animals. By his own natural standards, man wants a distinction to be made between good and evil. So if a man is taken to task for some wrongdoing it will be exactly what his own nature requires.

Material Blessings

"The righteous shall dwell amidst cool shades and fountains, and shall have fruits such as they desire; [They will be told], 'Eat and drink with relish in return for what you did [in life]: this is how We reward those who do good.' [But] woe on that Day to those who reject the truth! Eat [your fill] and enjoy your life for a little while, O you who are lost in sin. Woe on that Day to those who reject the truth! When they are bidden to bow down, they do not bow down. Woe on that Day to those who reject the truth! In which word then, after this, will they believe?" (*Al-Mursalat* 77:41-50)

In the present world, God has temporarily granted His blessings in order to put man to the test. In the hereafter, God's blessings will appear eternally in a more complete form. Today everyone shares in these blessings. But, in the hereafter, only those will have their share in these supreme blessings who submitted themselves to God in spite of their being free; who bowed down to God at a time when they were not compelled to do so. Those who bowed down on being called to God will earn Paradise, while those who bowed down only after seeing what a woeful fate awaited them will be consigned to Hell.

God and Man

• • •

"[O Prophet] forewarn them of the approaching Day, when hearts will leap up to the throats and choke them; when the wrongdoers will have no friend, nor any intercessor who will be listened to, [for] He is aware of the [most] stealthy glance, and of all that the hearts conceal. God will judge with [justice and] truth: but those whom they invoke besides Him, have no power to judge at all. Surely, God is all hearing, all seeing." (*Ghafir* 40:18-20)

In this present world all types of opportunities are available to a man. He is free to do what he likes. This makes a man fall a prey to misunderstanding. He comes to consider the present temporary state to be the permanent one, and fails to see that these opportunities available to a man are meant to test him and that they have not been given to him as a right. As soon as the test period is over, all these available opportunities will be snatched away from him. At that time man will come to realize his own powerlessness.

Man is of such a temperament that he wants to lead an unrestricted life. He therefore associates other things with God, so as to justify his wrongdoings. But on Doomsday, when the reality will come to light in its unveiled form, man will come to know there was none except God who had any real power.

"As for those who are mindful of God, they shall surely triumph: theirs shall be gardens and vineyards, and young maidens of equal age, and overflowing cups. There they shall not hear any idle talk, or any untruth: all this will be a recompense, a gift, that will suffice them, from your Lord, the Sustainer of the heavens and the earth and all that lies between them, the most Gracious [and] none shall have it in their power to raise their voices to Him. On the Day when the Spirit and the angels stand in ranks, no one will speak, except for those to whom the Lord of Mercy gives permission, and who will say only what is right. That Day is sure to come, so whoever wishes to, let him take the path that leads towards his Lord. We have warned you of a chastisement which is near at hand, on the Day when man shall [clearly] see what his hands have sent ahead, and when he who has denied the truth shall say, 'Oh, would that I were dust!'" (*Al-Naba'* 78:31-40)

The atmosphere of Paradise will be free of all kinds of absurdity and falsity, so only those will be chosen to dwell in the exquisite world of Paradise who gave proof of the fact in this world that they showed fervour in leading their lives far from things which were absurd and false.

No one will be admitted into Paradise on the basis of recommendation or on the basis of any kind of wishful thinking. Paradise is an exquisite haven. Entry to that world is predestined only for those who will reach there with exquisite souls. The present world is designed to select such an elite group. Only those who prove themselves to be eligible in this present world of trial will be entitled to enter Paradise.

The Sign of a Believer

"Remember God's favour to you, and the covenant, which He made with you when you said, 'We hear and we obey.' Fear God. God has full knowledge of the innermost thoughts of men. Believers, be steadfast in the cause of God and bear witness with justice. Do not let your enmity for others turn you away from justice. Deal justly; that is nearer to being God-fearing. Fear God. God is aware of all that you do."
(*Al-Ma'idah* 5:7-8)

Belief is a covenant which is made between God and His servant. In effect, man promises that he will lead his life in this world according to God's will. To fulfil his covenant, a man has to give proof of two things – one is his willingness to act upon the commandments of God, his whole existence responding at every moment in the most proper way – that of a servant before his Lord. When he looks at the universe, his mind should be filled with the concept of God's greatness and glory. When his feelings gush forth, they should do so forth for God. If he makes anything the centre of his attention his main focus should be on God. His love should be for God. His hopes and fears should be associated with God. God should become a part of his memory. He must obey and worship God. He must spend his wealth for God's cause.

The second condition of remaining steadfast on the covenant is his dealing justly with all people. Dealing justly means behaving with others exactly as they deserve in relation to the circumstances and, in all dealings following the truth rather than desires. In this regard, such caution should be exercised that when there is occasion to deal with on such occasions also when he is dealing with his enemies the path of justice should not be deviated from.

In this world, God appears in the form of signs, i.e., in form of such arguments as a man cannot reject. When God's evidence comes to a man and, instead of accepting it, he begins to argue he has rejected God's signs. Such a man will be severely punished by God, while those who have accepted it will be entitled to God's reward.

God's Friends

"Those who are close to God shall certainly have no fear, nor shall they grieve. For those who believe and are mindful of God, there is good news in this life and in the Hereafter: the Word of God shall never change. That is the supreme triumph."
(*Yunus* 10:62-64)

God's friends, according to the Quran, are not members of any mysterious group. These are known human beings and their qualities have been described in the above verses. These qualities are as follows:

They have faith, i.e., they come to have relations with God to a high degree of realization; they come to adopt that attitude in all affairs of their lives which comes into existence as a result of the fear of God. Those who come to possess these qualities in reality achieve a godly life in this world itself. With God's help, they come to follow the path which finally leads to Paradise. This happens according to a law of God which is immutable.

The word of God's friends is known to be of a religious nature in the same way as the word of believers and pious people.

Patience in the Face of Others' Oppression

"And why should we not put our trust in God when He has already guided us to our paths? We will, surely, bear with patience all the harm you do us. So in God let those who trust put their trust."
(*Ibrahim* 14:12)

All the prophets of God had to experience severe harm at the hands of their respective peoples. But the common attitude of all the prophets was one and the same and that was to continue to carry out peaceful *dawah* activities, with unconditional patience while enduring all the harm their people were causing them.

How can this be so? This is possible because *dawah* work is extremely positive in nature. But it can continue only where the caller and his listeners co-exist in a moderate environment. In order to maintain a consistently moderate environment, or peaceful atmosphere, all the prophets of God bore all things with unilateral patience. The fact is that it is patience which is the price of *dawah*. Where there is no patience, there can be no *dawah* activity.

In later periods also, those who want to do *dawah* work should adopt this attitude of patience in the full sense of the word.

How the Devil Misleads Us

"Then Satan said, 'Because You have put me in the wrong, I will lie in ambush for them on Your straight path: then I will surely come upon them from before them and from behind them and from their right and from their left, and then You will find most of them ungrateful.'" (*Al-A'raf* 7:16-17)

True believers will not be deceived by Satan. But those who are careless and unaware of the menace of Satan can be easily influenced by his temptation. We should never forget that Satan is our enemy and so we should treat him as an enemy. We should seek refuge in Allah so that Satanic temptation should not arise in our hearts.

We should always be most cautious, remain fully alert and endeavour to protect ourselves from Satan, otherwise we may easily be deceived by him.

The Quran says: "Surely Satan is your enemy: so treat him as an enemy: he calls on his followers only so that they should become inmates of the burning Fire." (35:6)

The Quran says that Satan misleads man through *tazin* or beautification. He beautifies evil and bad deeds and shows them as good and useful things. He presents evil in a beautiful manner and misleads him. This is the greatest weapon Satan has against man. The only way to save oneself from deception of Satan is constantly praying to God. The Quran mentions several prayers for this purpose. One of such prayers is as follows:

Allahuma inni awuzubika min hamazat ish shayateen. Wa awuzubik rabbi an yahdarun.

"My Lord, I seek refuge with You from the prompting of devils. I seek refuge with You, Lord, lest they should come near me." *(Al-Mu'minun* 23:97-98)

41

The World and the Hereafter

"Do not set up any other deity beside God, lest you incur disgrace, and be forsaken."
(*Al-Isra'* 17:72)

In this present world, divine realities have been veiled but in the hereafter, all these divine realities will come to light. God has endowed human beings with every kind of supreme ability and then settled them on the earth. Now the test of the believer is that he should make full use of his abilities and, by discovering veiled realities, make them the spiritual reservoir of his life. This for man spells success. And those who, in spite of having eyes, could not see God's glory, are as it were blind. Such people will be blind in the next world, because they remained blind in this world. They will be eternally deprived of their share in the blessings of the hereafter.

The Reality of Sacrifice

> "Their flesh and blood do not reach God: it is your piety that reaches Him. Thus God has subjected them to you, so that you may glorify Him for the guidance He has given you. Give glad tidings to those who do good."
> (*Al-Hajj* 22:37)

The act of sacrifice is performed on an animal, but it has been explained in this verse that what is desirable to God is in reality not the sacrifice of an animal but the sacrifice made by man himself. A man who slaughters an animal is in fact, saying in the language of action that he devotes himself to God's mission to the extent of sacrifice, and begs for his intention to be accepted.

The system of animal sacrifice has not been prescribed because God needs meat and blood. Sacrifice in actuality is a symbolic action. The sacrifice of an animal is an external picture of that man who has sacrificed himself to God. It is in fact one's own sacrifice which is in the form of the sacrifice of an animal. Fortunate are those for whom the sacrifice of animal culminates in self-sacrifice.

The act of sacrifice reminds believers of the readiness of the Prophet Ibrahim to give up his most beloved son. By sacrificing an animal, believers reaffirm their belief in Allah and pledge themselves to parting with their precious belongings, if there is a need for it. The Quran describes these sentiments in the following verse: "Truly, my prayers, my sacrifice, my life and my death all belong to Allah, the Lord of the Worlds." (*Al-An'am* 6:162)

Those Who Will Share in God's Mercy

"Do they imagine that the wealth and children We have provided have no other purpose except to help them in acquiring material benefits? No indeed. But they do not understand.

Those who tremble with fear of their Lord; and believe in His messages and do not ascribe partners to Him; and those who give to others what has been bestowed upon them with their hearts trembling at the thought that they must return to their Lord; it is they who vie with one another in doing good works and shall be the foremost in doing so."
(*Al-Mu'minun*, 23:55-61)

Those who are making worldly progress come to think that they are successful and that God's mercy is being showered on them. But material progress is not a sign that anyone is God's beloved servant and that God is showering mercy on him. In this world, material possessions are meant to put man to the test and are not meant as reward.

The sign of one's being granted the blessings of God in this world is that the events of the world come to remind him of God. While living in this world, one so blessed is experiencing fear and love of God. The world for him becomes a collection of such signs as permit him to see the glories of God. He comes to discover God in the form of such a Being who is above all types of polytheism. What he achieves in this world he regards as a direct gift from God, rather than the result of his personal ability. This feeling is so great within him that when he gives a part of his earnings to a needy man, he trembles with the feeling that he is not giving his wealth to him but is rather conveying a trust of God to one of God's servants. The fact always remains fresh in his mind that, one day or the other, he will die and be made to stand before God.

Those who live with such feelings are God's chosen people. This state of theirs is a sign that God's mercy is descending on them morning and evening. They are successful in this world and will be so in the hereafter.

What Does the Quran Say About Itself?

"Blessed be He who has revealed the criterion [the Quran] to His servant that he may warn the nations. Sovereign of the heavens and the earth, who has begotten no children and who has no partner in His sovereignty, it is He who has created all things and measured them out precisely."
(*Al-Furqan* 25:1-2)

We come to know from different statements of the Quran that this book has been sent for all nations of the world. A similar statement has been made regarding the Prophet in a number of places in the Quran. The following verse is one such example:

"We have sent you as a bearer of glad tidings and a warner for the whole of mankind, but most people have no knowledge."
(*Saba'* 34:28)

The Quran is written in Arabic, the language in which it was revealed in Arabia. But as far as its message is concerned it is, in its nature, entirely global and universal. It addresses all the nations of the world rather than any one particular nation.

The basic message of the Quran is that God is One. And it is clear that this is not any temporary or local matter. This is such a fact as concerns all human beings. It has been made clear in the Quran that a man does not die and end forever but that after his death he will be brought to life again and made to stand before God for the final reckoning. This is also such a reality as concerns the whole of humanity. Similarly, it has been enjoined in the Quran that we should adopt the path of justice in our dealings with others. This is also such a teaching as relates to all human beings. Moreover, it has been declared in the Quran that all human beings are the children of one and the same parents, i.e., Adam and Eve, and so all human beings are brothers and sisters to each other. If there is any difference, it is not on the basis of race but on degrees of piety. This is also such a teaching as relates to all human beings. Similarly, all the teachings of the Quran enjoy the position of universality. They provide guidance for all human beings from here to eternity.

Following One's Own Desires

> "Have you seen him who has taken his own desire to be his god? Can you be a guardian over him? Do you think most of them can hear or understand? They are like cattle. Indeed, they are even more astray."
> (*Al-Furqan* 25:43-44)

Taking someone or something to be one's deity means according him the greatest status. That person or thing assumes the greatest importance and all other things become unimportant. Man can ignore all other things but he cannot ignore that particular thing. That thing becomes so great in his eyes that all other things become valueless to him. When a man accords anything a higher status of such a kind, it is as if he has taken his own desire to be his deity. God created man. It is He who fulfils all of man's requirements. What a man receives in this world, he receives from God. Besides God, no one can give anything to anyone. It is a requirement of the status of God that man should regard Him as his all. Man should fear God the most and love Him the most. In his life the greatest status should be accorded to God. Besides Him, all things should become insignificant in his eyes. This is called monotheism and without monotheism no one can achieve salvation.

Those who take their desires to be their guide are just like animals. Animals cannot differentiate between truth and untruth. They know only their desires and follow them. If man descends to this level there will be no difference between him and an animal: it would be correct to say that such a man is worse than an animal, as the animal simply abides by his nature, whereas the human being has deviated from God's creation plan.

48

No Intercession

"Call upon those whom you set up beside God! They possess not an atom's weight either in the heavens or on the earth, nor have they any share in either, nor has He any helpers among them. No intercession avails with Him, except on the part of one to whom He grants permission. When their hearts are relieved of fear, they will enquire from those to whom permission is granted, 'What has your Lord said?' They will answer, 'The truth. He is the Most High, the Supreme One.'" (*Saba'* 34:22-23)

Most people's attitude to such faith is self-styled and this makes them fearless of the grip of the hereafter. They make the supposition that certain personalities have so great a status with God that their interceding with God can cause their sins to be forgiven.

But faith of this kind is not only baseless but is also an underestimation of the divinity of God. One who attains a true realization of God will yield to final extent, with the feeling of God's greatness. How strange it is to think that some other human being can effectively bring about one's salvation. If in the hereafter God grants permission to anyone to speak, he will say whatever God will have already decided upon, rather than try to persuade Him to accede to his requests.

The Trial of Prosperity

"For it has been thus whenever We sent a warner to any community. Its affluent ones said, 'We reject what you have been sent with.' They say, 'We have more wealth and children; and we are surely not going to be punished.' Say to them, 'My Lord increases the provision for whoever He pleases and decreases it for whoever He pleases; but most people do not know it.' It is not your wealth or your children that will confer on you nearness to Us. It is those who believe and act righteously who will be doubly rewarded for their good deeds, and will dwell in peace in the high pavilions [of paradise], while those who strive to thwart Our messages, seeking to defeat their purpose, shall be summoned to punishment." (*Saba'* 34:34-38)

Those who come to possess power and wealth achieve a position of greatness in this present world. This creates false confidence in them. Then, when such people are warned of the hereafter, they do not attach any importance to it. They do not believe that God will dishonour them in the hereafter while He has honoured them in this world.

This same false trust has been the greatest cause of the affluent class not accepting the truth. And when affluent people despise something the lower classes also come to look down upon it. Thus both the upper and lower classes are turned away from accepting the truth.

The possessions of this world are only meant to put man to the test and are not rewards. The increase in wealth and other material objects is not a sign of being close to God, nor is any decrease in these things a sign of not being close to Him. Only those will find a place close to God who can prove that they have lived with the remembrance that what they have has been granted to them by God and who have remained within the limits laid down for them by God. Such are the people who will be entitled to the eternal reward of God in the hereafter.

Light and Darkness

"The blind and the sighted are not equal, nor are the darkness and the light; shade and heat are not alike, nor are the living and the dead. God causes whom He will to hear Him, but you cannot make those who are in their graves hear you. You are but a warner." (*Fatir* 35:19-23)

It is a fact that what can be expected from light cannot be expected from darkness. Similarly, what can be had from shade cannot be had from the sun. The same is true of human beings. Among human beings, some are blind and some are sighted. The sighted recognizes his path immediately. But the blind will forever stray. He will never recognize his path.

What is meant by faith is realization. God's desired faith is that which is achieved as a discovery. Potentially, every man has the ability to have this realization within him. But only those avail of this ability who have the courage to reach their destination by crossing the horizon of realization.

The Blessings of Paradise

"This is a Reminder. The righteous shall have a good place to return to: the Gardens of eternity with gates thrown wide open to them. They will be comfortably seated; reclining, they will call for abundant fruit and drink; with them, they will have pure, modest women of an equal age. This is what you were promised on the Day of Reckoning: Our provision for you will never be exhausted."
(*Sad* 38:49-54)

In the hereafter, the doors of Paradise will be opened to those who keep the doors of their hearts opened for acceptance of the truth; to those who come to fear God before God appears before them. These are the fortunate people who will share in the eternal blessings of the next world.

The blessings of the hereafter mentioned in the Quran are apparently the same as those enjoyed by human beings in this world. But there is a great difference between the two. That is to say, blessings are granted in this world in their temporary and initial form but, in the hereafter, these blessings will be given in their eternal and final form. Moreover, every type of fear and anxiety associated with these supreme blessings will be terminated, something which is not possible at all in this present world.

Man and Satan

• • •

"Your Lord said to the angels, 'I am about to create a human being out of clay; and when I have formed him fully and breathed My spirit into him, prostrate yourselves before him.' Thereupon the angels prostrated themselves, all of them together, but not Satan, who was too proud. He became one of those who deny the truth. God said, 'Satan, what prevented you from prostrating yourself to what I created with My own Hands? Were you overcome by arrogance, or are you of those who think [only] of themselves as exalted?' Satan replied, 'I am better than him. You created me from fire, but You created him from clay.' 'Begone! You are accursed: My curse will remain upon you till the Day of Judgement!'"
(*Sad* 38:71-78)

God created man as an extremely special creature and, as a sign of this, He commanded the jinn and angels to prostrate themselves before him. When it happened subsequently that Iblis did not prostrate himself before Adam, he was declared the accursed one forever. This was a very serious event which was significant not just for Iblis, but also for Adam.

By refusing to bow down before Adam, Iblis became the eternal enemy of Adam's progeny. Human history started on a new dimension from the very first day.

This event decided that the life journey of human being would not be a simple matter but rather one of extreme arduousness. He would have to establish himself on the right path, while fighting Iblis's temptations and his deceitful tricks, all the way, otherwise he would reach his destination safely.

Satan's deception stands between man and paradise. Those who protect themselves from the deceit of Satan will enter into the eternal gardens of paradise, but those who fail to unveil Satan's deceit will be deprived of paradise.

The Cautious Temperament

"Believers, if an evil-doer brings you news, ascertain the correctness of the report fully, lest you unwittingly harm others, and then regret what you have done, and know that the Messenger of God is among you. If he were to obey you in many things, you would suffer for it. However, God has endeared the faith to you, and beautified it in your hearts, and has made denial of the truth, wickedness, and disobedience hateful to you. People such as these are rightly guided through God's bounty and favour; God is all knowing, and wise." (*Al-Hujurat*, 49:6-8)

When anyone is informed of another's wrongdoing, believing in such news as a matter of hearsay is entirely against the spirit of faith. It is compulsory for the recipient of this news to make proper unbiased enquiries about it and only form his opinions after satisfying himself that the news is correct.

It often happens that when someone is given bad news, he immediately accepts it and begins to plan retaliatory action. This is extremely irresponsible behaviour. Neither should a man form an opinion on the basis of such news before making enquiries nor should he advise others to take any action.

Those who tread the right path eventually develop an extremely cautious temperament. They come to abhor accusing others. They prefer remaining silent to voicing disapproval on the basis of mere allegations. Such a temperament is a sign of their having received their share of God's mercy. The faith they declare with their tongues is actually resonating in their lives.

At the Time of Dispute

●●●

"If two parties of believers fight against each other, make peace between them; then if after that one of them transgresses against the other, fight the party that transgresses until it submits to the command of God. Then if it complies, make peace between them with equity, and act justly. Truly, God loves the just. Surely all believers are brothers. So make peace between your brothers, and fear God, so that mercy may be shown to you." (*Al-Hujurat* 49:9-10)

The answer to how the believers should live with each other is, in a word, that they should live in the way that brothers live with each other. A religious relationship is in no way superior to a blood relationship. If two believers choose to fight against each other, they should not keep adding fuel to the fire between them but should rather make peace between them as a matter of brotherly feeling.

When two believers come to fight against each other, the right Islamic way to resolve the issue is to carry out an enquiry into the actual matter then support should be extended to the one who is in the right and the one who is in the wrong should be compelled to agree with the fair decision arrived at.

Wealth and Children

$\bullet\bullet\bullet$

"O believers! Do not let your wealth or your children distract you from remembrance of God. Those who do so will be the losers. And spend out of what We have provided you with before death comes to one of you and he says, 'My Lord! If only You would grant me respite for a little while, then I would give alms and be among the righteous.' But God will not grant a reprieve to a soul when its appointed time has come; God is well-aware of what you do."
(*Al-Munafiqun* 63:9-11)

The subject of the hereafter is one of the greatest concern for everybody. But wealth and children distract a man from this. A man should know that wealth and children are not goals in life: they are resources. They are granted to human beings so that they may devote them to God's cause, thus using them to build their hereafter. But the foolish man comes to consider them to be the goals. When such as he reach their final end they will not find anything there except regret. Wealth and children and other material things of this type which a man is granted in this world are not rewards for him: they are a trial, i.e. it does not mean that a man on being granted these things should make a luxurious life for himself and remain engrossed in it; each of these things is rather a test paper for man, and should be taken as such rather than as a blessing. Blessings will be granted in the hereafter. The present world is the place for trial and the hereafter is the place for receiving rewards or punishments according to man's performance in that trial.

Sublimity of Character

●●●

"*Nun* By the pen, and all that they write! By the grace of your Lord, you are not a mad man. Most surely, you will have a never ending reward. For you are truly of a sublime character. Soon you will see, as will they, which of you is a prey to madness. Your Lord knows best who has fallen by the wayside, and who has remained on the true path." (*Al-Qalam* 68:1-7)

Sublimity of character means a man's actions being superior to the behaviour of others. He does not wrong those who wrong him or do good to those who do good to him. He rather does good to all others whether they behave badly with him or not. The Prophet possessed the latter kind of character, proving that he was a man of principle. His personality was not the product of the circumstances but rather of his own high principles. This sublime character of the prophet is quite in accordance with his claim that he was the messenger of God.

What is meant by 'the pen and all that men write' is historical record. As a record, the Quran is the most exceptional book in human memory. It was compiled in the form of history and the man to whom the Quran was revealed was an equally exceptional personality. The uniqueness of this event can be explained only if the Quran be accepted as God's book and Muhammad as the messenger of God. The Quran's being preserved in an exceptional and complete way and the fulfilling of the teachings of the Prophet, which have stood up to every historical test, could never have been possible without God's special help.

Human Behaviour

"O man, having striven hard towards your Lord, you shall meet Him: he who is given his record in his right hand shall have an easy reckoning and he shall return to his people, joyfully, but as for him whose record shall be given to him from behind his back, he will pray for utter destruction and he will enter the blazing flame. He used to be happy with his own people; for he never thought that he would have to return [to God]." (*Al-Inshiqaq* 84:6-14)

There are two ways of leading one's life. One of them is to be serious about reality. One who is sincere about this will necessarily become a responsible person. He will live in a state of concern, as he will fear that if he is deprived of God's mercy, nothing will await him except eternal punishment. On the contrary, one who is not serious about reality will lead a life of thoughtlessness. He, being negligent of tomorrow's end, will remain engrossed in today's interests.

Those who are engrossed in today's luxuries and comforts will be neglectful of tomorrow's end and will then experience the dreadful consequences of this negligence in the hereafter. On the contrary, those who are anxious about tomorrow will treat this world as a place in which to pay their dues rather than a place in which to acquire and indulge in luxuries. And the end of these opposite kinds of people cannot be the same.

The Greater Success

"Those who persecute the believing men and believing women, and then do not repent, will surely suffer the punishment of Hell, and the torment of burning. But those who believe and do good deeds shall be rewarded with gardens watered by flowing rivers. That is the supreme triumph. The grip of your Lord is indeed severe—it is He who begins and repeats [His creation]—and He is the Forgiving and Loving One. The Lord of the Glorious Throne, Executor of His own will."
(*Al-Buruj* 85:10-16)

It is undoubtedly a crime if a man is shown the truth and he does not accept it. But the greater crime is to become the enemy of the caller of truth, to hatch conspiracies against him and to speak out and take action against him. Such people will be debarred from God's mercy for ever.

On the contrary, those who on hearing the call of truth immediately accept it and mould their lives upon it and, by supporting the caller of truth, make their mission strong, will receive their reward in the form of God's endless mercy. They will abide in the eternal gardens of the hereafter.

The Spirit of Fasting

To those who say, 'God has commanded us not to believe in any messenger unless he brings down to us an offering to be consumed by fire,' say, 'Messengers before me have come to you with clear signs, including the one you demand. Why did you kill them, if you are telling the truth?' If they deny you, so have other messengers been denied before you, who came with clear signs, scriptures and enlightening book. Every human being is bound to taste death: and you shall receive your rewards in full on the Day of Resurrection. He who is kept away from the Fire and is admitted to Paradise, will surely triumph; for the life of this world is nothing but an illusory enjoyment.

You will surely be tried and tested in your possessions and your persons, and you shall surely hear many hurtful things from those who were given the Book before you and from those who set up partners with God, but if you endure with fortitude and restrain yourselves, that indeed is a matter of strong determination. (*Al-Baqarah*, 2:183-186)

Fasting was not prescribed only for the followers of last Prophet. Fasting is such a form of worship as has been prescribed in the religion of the earlier prophets also.

As it is amply clear from the above verses, that fasting has many benefits. The most important of them is that it instils piety, or the fear of God in a man. What is fear of God? It is the feeling that accompanies the belief that everything is the gift of God. When He wills, He will deprive man of His gifts. The fasting of Ramadan is an annual period of training calculated to produce this same feeling. In this month, a man on his own, temporarily abstains from eating and drinking. In this way, overwhelmed by hunger and thirst, he has the experience of how great problem he will have to face if God were to deprive him of food and drink permanently. This feeling engenders in him an inner divine state which has been described as piety in the Quran.

The next most important virtue fasting produces in a man is the spirit of thanksgiving. A man remains hungry and thirsty all day until evening comes. He remains in this state until the sun sets. Now he breaks his fast and he eats and drinks to his fill.

This custom of breaking the fast is as an experience that reminds a man of the reality of how great a blessing God has given to mankind in the form of food and water. And this experience of a blessing reminds a man of all the other blessings of God. He then filled with gratitude.

The third quality which fasting infuses into a man is the spirit of prayer. The month of Ramadan is the month of spiritual training for the one keeping the fast. In this month a man, by bearing the trials of hunger and thirst, subdues the material aspect of his existence and develops its non-material aspect. The frequency of prayer awakens in him the feeling of total devotion to God. By reciting and listening to the Quran, he comes to understand its meanings. And the consciousness of God's greatness is awakened in him. Thus he comes to fear, thank and glorify God.

In this way, fasting enables a man to pray to God with sincerity. His prayer becomes one full of feeling; his prayer becomes that of a questing man; his prayer becomes the invocation of a man who has come very close to God.

What is the Importance of Praying to God?

> "Recite what has been revealed to you of the book, and pray regularly. Surely prayer restrains one from indecency and evil and remembrance of God is greater. God has knowledge of all your actions."
> (*Al-'Ankabut* 29:45)

In this verse the sentence 'Surely prayer restrains one from indecency and evil' is the recognition of prayer rather than simply the result of prayer. The second sign of true prayer is that with it remembrance of God should become uppermost in the suppliant's feelings. And the remembrance of God is undoubtedly the greatest of all the virtues.

Prayer does not just have an external form but also an internal spirit. Whenever the spirit of prayer enters into the life of the worshipper. Certain cardinal virtues manifest themselves in him. The repetition of 'Allah is great' in prayer makes him feel small and insignificant. The recitation of the Quran in prayer awakens the consciousness of God in him. Bowing down and self-prostration in prayer engender in him the feeling of humility.

Observing prayer behind an *Imam* teaches him the lesson of sociability. To say 'Peace and the blessings of God be upon you' at the end of prayer arouses in him the sentiment that the feeling of peace and blessings should well up in his heart for all the people of the world.